Charley Waters Goes to Gettysburg

SUSAN SINNOTT

PHOTOGRAPHS BY DOROTHY HANDELMAN

THE MILLBROOK PRESS   BROOKFIELD, CONNECTICUT

photograph on pages 42–43 courtesy of Ken Schwartz

Library of Congress Cataloging-in-Publication Data
Sinnott, Susan
Charley Waters goes to Gettysburg / Susan Sinnott :
photographs by Dorothy Handelman.
p.   cm.
ISBN 0-7613-1567-5 (lib. bdg.)
1. Gettysburg (Pa.), Battle of, 1863 Juvenile literature.
2. Historical reenactments—Pennsylvania—Gettysburg
Juvenile literature. I. Handelman, Dorothy, ill. II. Title.
E475.53.S56 2000
973.7'349—dc21 99-36119 CIP

Published by The Millbrook Press, Inc.
2 Old New Milford Road
Brookfield, Connecticut 06804
www.millbrookpress.com

ACKNOWLEDGMENTS

To Nathaniel, the real-life Charley, for his love of time travel, and to Lucy, a travel companion for any era   —SS

To my family, with love
                    —DH

In some ways this book seemed to create itself in four full days at Gettysburg, Pennsylvania, in July 1998. But of course nothing happens without lots of support and good will. Many thanks go to Marcia Leonard, who walked Susan through the process of turning an idea into a book and who just happened to know of a talented and willing photographer. We were surely boosted, too, by the unflagging enthusiasm of Laura Walsh, our editor at The Millbrook Press. We also owe a debt of gratitude to the 69th Pennsylvania for their helpfulness, knowledge, and good humor. Also to the Kopich family, especially Ryan and John, for letting us follow them around, through good times and bad. Thanks to John Wackman for maneuvering the RV (and its passengers) in and out of tight places, to Lucy for carrying and guarding the camera equipment, and to Nathaniel for getting us to Gettysburg in the first place.

My name is Charley Waters and I live near Philadelphia, Pennsylvania. I'm eight years old and have just finished third grade. In my normal life I play soccer, fight with my sister, and have to be told more than once to clean my room.

I have another life, though. In my other life, I never have to be told twice to do anything. I follow orders, no matter what. In my other life, I'm in the army and I'm fighting in the Civil War. My dad and I are Civil War reenactors; it's our hobby. We dress the way soldiers did in the 1860s. We sleep in canvas tents and eat soldiers' rations, or food. We follow the orders of the officers in charge, just the way real soldiers do. In the army, disobeying an officer can get you into big trouble.

My dad was the first to enlist, or sign up. He is a private with the 69th Pennsylvania VI, Company D, Army of the Potomac—another name for the Union army. The 69th was a real regiment, or part of the army, and its soldiers were Irishmen from Philadelphia.

They call me a private, too, although I'm too young to carry a gun or even to be on the battlefield during a reenactment. Still I get to go along with the regiment to famous battle sites—places like Bull Run, near Manassas, Virginia; Antietam, in Maryland; and, of course, Gettysburg, Pennsylvania.

When I step into my Civil War life, I live in a different time and place. I am a completely different me. Sometimes I'm not sure which me is the real me.

This summer will be the 135th anniversary of the Battle of Gettysburg. There will be a reenactment of Pickett's Charge. It will be full-scale, which means there will be as many men pretending to fight as really fought—about thirty thousand. My dad and I are going, of course, and my mom and my sister, too.

The men of the 69th Pennsylvania are very proud of their role in the Battle of Gettysburg. The Civil War, also called the War Between the States, had been going on for more than two years when the fighting came to Gettysburg. Both the Union army, called Yankees, who fought for the North, and the Confederate army, called Rebels, who fought for the South, had won battles. In the spring of 1863 the leader of the Confederate army, General Robert E. Lee, believed his troops were ready to march out of Virginia and fight on Yankee soil. In June they entered Pennsylvania, and on July 1 they went into the small town of Gettysburg looking for shoes. They didn't find any shoes, but they did run into part of the Union army. The battle that followed lasted for three days. After the first day, the Rebs were ahead. On the second day, however, they had to give up the high ground to the Yankees. In a big battle it is important to get the high ground and never give it up, and that's what the Yankees did. On the third day the Yankees held the high ground during Pickett's Charge. This was the most important part of the Battle of Gettysburg, and the 69th Pennsylvania played a very important role. They stood at a place called the Angle and turned the Rebels away. If the Yankees hadn't held that day, the Confederate army probably would have won the battle. They would have then gone to Washington and then possibly farther north, and maybe even have won the war.

The 69th Pennsylvania, along with the other Irish regiments, became famous for fighting hard and for being brave. When the Civil War began, most of the soldiers in the 69th had just come to this country from Ireland and were very poor. Some enlisted to get food, and others enlisted to thank America for helping the people of Ireland when they were starving during the great famine.

What's even more special about this year is that my dad and I will bring the regimental colors—that is, the flag that tells everyone we are part of the 69th Pennsylvania. It's a green flag with a gold harp on it, and at the end of Pickett's Charge, it was still waving proudly.

We pack the flag very carefully. Then we get out the big wooden trunk that holds our gear, and I get my uniform from my closet and pack it, too. Sometimes I wonder, what if we lost the flag?

How would the 69th go into Pickett's Charge without the flag to follow? Don't worry, my dad says, we'll get it there safely. Those were our orders, and soldiers must always follow orders.

As we drive to Gettysburg we sing Irish songs from the Civil War to get into the spirit. My favorite is called "My Father's Gun," and we sing it at the top of our lungs. It tells the story of Paddy McKee who brings his father's gun on the boat from Ireland and uses it when he fights in the Civil War. "And oh what fun," starts the chorus, "To see them run and to leave our name in story-o; with my father's gun I'll follow the drum and fight my way to glory-o!"

Maybe I'm imagining it, but I think I can hear the drums even before we get to Gettysburg.

By the time we arrive many reenactors have already been in the camp for a day or two. They are busy running errands and some are even looking for new recruits. They're happy to see my dad and me, and they make us feel welcome. Dad takes the regimental colors to the officers' camp, and then we head to our camp, which is for enlisted soldiers. My mom and sister will stay in town this time.

We love putting on our uniforms and staying in them day after day, just like real soldiers. We find the small boxwood tree our unit has brought along and we break off a sprig. Irish soldiers used to put boxwood in their hats to remind them of the green of Ireland.

My dad puts up his tent,
and then I put up mine.
I take my gear out of my
haversack and roll out
my blanket.

Just as I'm finishing up, my friend Ryan comes by. He's also part of the 69th Pennsylvania, and we like to be together during the big events. We know other kids from other regiments, too.

After we're settled, there is a little time to walk around and see other soldiers. There are thousands of them from all over the United States and even from other countries. The Union camp is separate from the Confederate camp but not so far away that we don't see a Reb from time to time.

When we pass by the officers' camp, we see the regimental colors. It's good to know we got the flag to Gettysburg safe and sound.

It's hot and humid, just as it was during the real battle. This makes a soldier sweat in these wool uniforms. Some of the men worry that the heat will be too much for them.

The kids just worry about doing the right thing. My dad tells us some of the things we're supposed to do to get ready for the first battle tomorrow. We must listen to him and do what he says.

This will be one of the biggest Civil War reenactments ever. There are long lines at the big red barn where the reenactors must register. There are also long lines for water and for rides on the hay wagons that will bring us to parts of the battle site. The scratchy wool uniforms, the long dresses, and the heat make us all tired and a little grumpy.

We feel better when night comes. Both women and men begin to cook supper, and we all look forward to a good sleep tonight. When the sun goes down, I play my harmonica for a while and then get ready to go to sleep. We're tired from all we've done today and excited about the first battle bright and early tomorrow.

Dad and I think that morning is the most special time in camp. As soon as I wake up, I hear the men's low voices and the swishing of the women's long skirts. I can smell breakfast cooking over a campfire. It's early, but we always get up early at camp—especially on the day of a battle.

Even though we're going into battle in a few hours, Dad makes me brush my teeth. I have a toothbrush made of bone, just the way soldiers did. I wonder if real soldier boys had to brush their teeth when the enemy was nearby and ready to fight.

We watch our friend Gunter, who is reenacting the role of a war illustrator. Gunter shaves his head in the morning. Gunter is from Germany. Many of the real Civil War illustrators were German, too.

This morning's fight will be the battle of Little Round Top. It took place on the second day of the real battle. Before this battle the men talk about what will happen and who should pretend to die in the battle. Of course no one wants to die, but the battle won't seem very realistic if everyone just keeps fighting until the end. It's better to decide beforehand who will fall and in what order. My dad always hates to hear he'll be one of the first to die, especially in an important battle. But he knows everyone has to take his turn.

By nine o'clock all the soldiers and musicians are ready for inspection. This is my dad. Everything he wears, even his glasses, is exactly right for 1863.

The musicians begin to play. One of the officers gives last orders to the other men. Then they cheer and fire their guns in the air. This is called "capping off."

They begin to march to the battle-field. Everyone, including my dad, is excited to be going to the first battle.

Ryan and I find a place to watch just at the edge of the woods.

We see Gunter, who is sketching as the men take their positions.

Then the cannons begin to fire! Union lines move toward the Rebs.

We feel excited and nervous as we watch the smoke and blue uniforms. We can't tell who is who. Even though we already know who will win the battle, we don't know who will fall and "die." We all know it's make-believe, but it seems so real that we can't help being a little worried. When we look out at the battlefield and then at the other spectators, we know we're not the only ones.

Finally the smoke clears, and we see the men coming back toward us. We've won the battle! The Union has held Little Round Top! Our men are happy, but tired. Most walk slowly back to camp. I try to keep up with them.

Some stop to talk to new friends.

Just after we've reached our camp, a boy about my age from another unit camped near ours jumps into the path and shouts, "Time for the little kids' battle!" Of course, all the kids are ready at once. We love to have our own battle. I play dead for a while, but then some older kids come over and shake me back to life!

Later that afternoon, after we've had lunch and Dad's had a rest, we head over to the sutler area. "Sutler" is the name for the people who used to follow soldiers from battle to battle and sell them things they needed. At reenactments, sutlers set up stands near the public viewing area. I like to go sutlering as often as possible. My mom and dad let me buy one new toy at every reenactment.

The first stop is the post office. But there's already a young Reb there!

To get to the sutler area, we walk through the civilian camp. That's where families stay who are reenactors but aren't part of the military. We know some of the families who are staying there.

This girl is using a schoolbook from the 1860s.

This year my dad and I decided to get our picture taken at one of the old-fashioned photo studios. We thought this one would be just right. Then I had my picture taken alone. Don't I look serious? Like a real soldier. Dad says I look like Paddy McKee from the song "My Father's Gun."

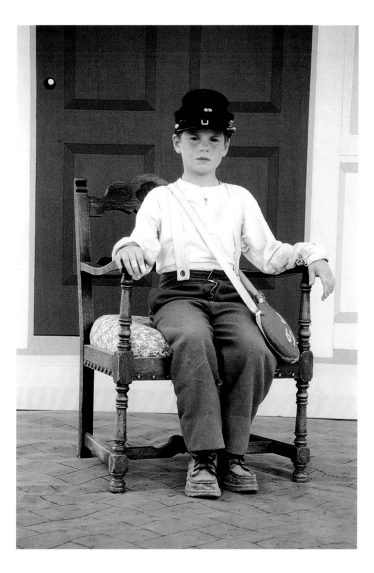

Afterward, I start looking for my toy. This is one of my favorite sutlers because it has lots of toy soldiers.

We walk back to camp even though it's a long way. It's nice to get back. My mom is there, and she wants to play checkers. She tries hard to beat me but never can.

After checkers there's a little time before dinner, so I practice whittling. This is something soldiers did to take their minds off the next day's battle.

Tomorrow is Pickett's Charge. It may have been the biggest and most famous attack of the entire Civil War, but it must have been the scariest, too. At the real camp the men must have looked around at each other and wondered which of them would still be alive tomorrow at this time. But what could they do? They had to follow orders. Maybe they did the same things our men do the night before a big battle: listen to music, look at the campfire, and try not to worry too much about tomorrow.

Now it's the last day and time for the last battle: Pickett's Charge. Everyone who comes to Gettysburg learns about Pickett's Charge. Like the other battles, we already know how today will turn out. We know that General Robert E. Lee will order the Rebs under General George Pickett—three divisions of thirteen thousand men—to charge across an open field right toward our Union lines. When the gunpowder is all gone, the men will fight each other hand to hand.

We know, too, that by the end of that day, July 3, 1863, Pickett will have no brigade left. And the Rebs will never again be as strong as they were before the Battle of Gettysburg. In all, more than fifty thousand Union and Confederate soldiers died over the three days. It's sad. And it's the sadness that people think of, mostly.

This morning begins as the others have: breakfast, dress call, and then march. Not far away the Rebs do the same. Everyone looks tired and nervous.

When I watch the 69th leave to take up their position, it doesn't make any difference that I know what will happen. It doesn't matter that no one will really die or that history won't change. Reenacting is about pretending, or time travel, as some of the men like to say. I think I know what they mean. I think I know what it's really like to see my dad go into a battle that he might not survive.

The reenactors who aren't taking part in the battle sit on a grassy area near camp. From there we can see the men take their positions. We can also see across the battlefield to the public viewing area. But we really only pay attention to the men in blue.

The cannonade seems to last forever! Just like the day of the real battle, Confederate cannons blast Union lines for a long time—more than an hour! Then the Reb soldiers start to move. They walk silently, without making the Rebel yell we all are used to hearing.

The smoke is so thick, it's hard to see. I stand up and watch the green flag wave at the Angle. I can barely stand the excitement. I can see the blue and gray meet. I can hear the guns and see the swords flashing.

Then the Rebs begin to retreat. Our regimental colors are still waving! The battle is over, and the ground is full of dead soldiers. We're relieved to see those men stand up and walk away, too.

It's a proud day for the Irish of Philadelphia and for all of the Union. It's a sad day for the Rebs. I can't help but feel bad for them. Walking past their camp day after day and seeing their proud cavalry, I sometimes think of them as friends. After all, we share a love for history and for the Civil War.

By the time we get back to camp many people have packed up and are ready to go home. It's time to say good-bye. Where will we see each other next? At Antietam, Manassas, or maybe Vicksburg?

Soon I'll change from my uniform into civilian clothes. Then I'll go back to my normal life. But before we get the car to pack up, my dad and I take one last walk together. Dad says he doesn't think he'll ever see anything like today's action again in his life. He thinks that maybe none of us will. I'm not so sure. I'm only eight. I have many years of the Civil War ahead of me.

GLOSSARY

Brigade: A military unit made up of three or four *regiment*s. Usually three brigades make up a division.

Cannonade: A long period of heavy cannon fire.

Capping off: A safety precaution, whereby *reenactors* clear their rifles of any obstructions or gunpowder at the beginning or end of a battle. (Leftover gunpowder can ignite.)

Cavalry: A military unit mounted on horseback.

Civilian: An ordinary citizen, rather than someone in the military.

Confederate: A supporter of the Confederate States of America, which consisted of the eleven Southern states that seceded, or split, from the *Union* during the Civil War.

Enlist: To enter the military by choice.

Famine: A serious food shortage, often causing widespread starvation.

Haversack: A one-strap canvas shoulder bag used for carrying supplies.

Private: The lowest rank in the army during the Civil War. After *enlisting*, this was usually the first rank a soldier would hold.

Rations: A fixed amount of food given to soldiers.

Rebels: The name given to *Confederate* soldiers during the Civil War.

Recruits: New members of the military.

Reenactor: Someone who acts out a historical event.

Regiment: A basic unit of soldiers during the Civil War. At the beginning of the war a regiment generally consisted of 1,000 troops. By the Battle of Gettysburg, however, regiments had dwindled to 300–400 troops.

Regimental colors: A flag that is unique to a particular *regiment*. "Colors" usually refers to a single flag.

Sutler: Someone who follows military units from camp to camp and sells them supplies.

Union: The United States, especially during the Civil War.

Yankee: A *Union* soldier during the Civil War.

FURTHER READING

Brill, Marlene Targ. *Diary of a Drummer Boy*. Brookfield, CT: The Millbrook Press, 1996.

Carter, Alden R. *The Battle of Gettysburg*. New York: Franklin Watts, 1990.

Clinton, Catherine. *Life in Civil War America*. The National Park Civil War Series, 1996.

Damon, Duane. *When This Cruel War Is Over*: *The Civil War Homefront*. Minneapolis: Lerner, 1996.

Dolan, Edward F. *The American Civil War: A House Divided*. Brookfield, CT: The Millbrook Press, 1997.

Gay, Kathlyn, and Martin Gay. *Voices from the Past: The Civil War*. New York: Twenty-First Century Books, 1995.

Hakim, Joy. *War, Terrible War*. From "A History of US" series. New York: Oxford University Press, 1994.

Haskins, Jim. *The Day Fort Sumter Was Fired On: A Photo History of the Civil War*. New York: Scholastic, 1995.

Meltzer, Milton, ed. *Voices from the Civil War*. New York: Harper Trophy, 1989.

Mettger, Zak. *Till Victory Is Won: Black Soldiers in the Civil War*. New York: Lodestar/Dutton, 1994.

Morrison, Taylor. *Civil War Artist*. Boston: Houghton Mifflin, 1999.

Murphy, Jim. *The Boys' War: Confederate and Union Soldiers Talk About the Civil War*. New York: Clarion, 1990.

Murphy, Jim. *The Long Road to Gettysburg*. New York: Clarion, 1992.

Polacco, Patricia. *Pink and Say*. New York: Philomel, 1994.

Ray, Delia. *Behind the Blue and Gray: The Soldier's Life in the Civil War*. Part of "The Young Reader's History of the Civil War" series. New York: Lodestar, 1991.

Robertson, James I., Jr. *Civil War! America Becomes One Nation*. New York: Knopf, 1992.

Smith, Carter, ed. *1863: The Crucial Year*. Brookfield, CT: The Millbrook Press, 1993.

Stolz, Mary. *A Ballad of the Civil War*. New York: HarperCollins, 1997.

Ward, Geoffrey C., Ken Burns, and Ric Burns. *The Civil War: An Illustrated History*. New York: Knopf, 1990.

Zeinert, Karen. *Those Courageous Women of the Civil War*. Brookfield, CT: The Millbrook Press, 1998.